The REAL KAMA SUTRA

by The Odd Squad

(AND ALLAN PLENDERLEITH)

RAVETTE PUBLISHING

THE ODD SQUAD and all related characters
©2001 by Allan Plenderleith

All rights reserved.

First Published by Ravette Publishing Limited 2001
Reprinted 2001, 2002, 2003, 2004, 2005, 2006

This book is sold subject to the condition that
it shall not, by way of trade or otherwise, be
lent, resold, hired out or otherwise circulated
without the publisher's prior consent in any
form of binding or cover other than that in
which this is published and without a similar
condition including this condition being
imposed on the subsequent purchaser.

Printed and bound for
Ravette Publishing Limited,
Unit 3, Tristar Centre
Star Road, Partridge Green
West Sussex RH13 8RA

by Gutenberg Press, Malta

ISBN 10: 1-84161-103-4
ISBN 13: 978-1-84161-103-7

No. 1
THE 'TURN OFF THE LIGHTS TO HIDE THE FLAB' POSITION.

THE 'QUICK BONK'.

No. 3
THE 'HOW TO <u>REALLY</u> SATISFY A WOMAN IN BED' POSITION.

THE 'TANGLED UP IN SAGGY BOOBS' POSITION.

No. 5
THE 'WOMAN GOES ON TOP FOR A CHANGE' POSITION.

THE 'SHOULDN'T HAVE HAD THAT CURRY' POSITION.

THE 'CAN'T DO IT IF THE DOG'S WATCHING' POSITION.

THE 'MOVE YOUR BUM, I'M TRYING TO WATCH EASTENDERS' POSITION.

No. 9
THE 'SHOULDN'T HAVE GONE AT IT FOR 9 HOURS LAST NIGHT' POSITION.

THE 'DRANK TOO MUCH AND FELL ASLEEP' POSITION.

THE 'SHOULDN'T HAVE LOST THE KEYS TO THE HANDCUFFS' POSITION.

THE 'WITHDRAWING JUST AS YOU CLIMAX' MOVE.

THE 'SUSPENDERS SNAP DURING YOUR SEXY DANCE' MOVE.

THE 'TRYING TO CONVINCE THE POLICEMAN THAT THESE ARE ACTUALLY AIRBAGS' POSITION.

No. 15
THE 'LIGHT UP AFTER SEX' MOVE.

THE 'LET'S NOT WAIT SO LONG UNTIL THE NEXT TIME' POSITION.

No. 17
THE 'LET'S KEEP THE LIGHT <u>ON</u> DURING SEX' POSITION.

A WOMAN'S GUIDE TO A MAN'S EROGENOUS ZONES!

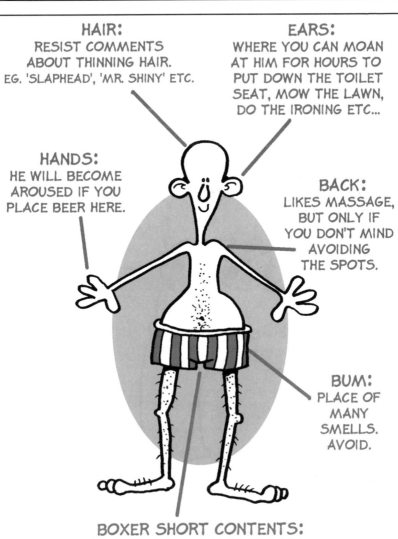

A MAN'S GUIDE TO A WOMAN'S EROGENOUS ZONES!

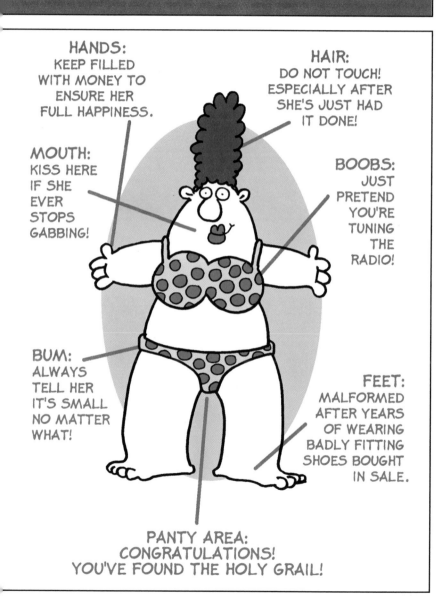

NEVER CONFUSE THE ELECTRIC TOOTHBRUSH WITH YOUR VIBRATOR!

SEX TIP No. 2
LADIES – TO ATTRACT MEN, TRY THE NEW PERFUME THAT PROVES IRRESISTIBLE!

SEX TIP No. 3
TO GIVE THE ILLUSION OF AN ACTIVE SEX LIFE, SIMPLY KNOCK HOLES BEHIND YOUR HEADBOARD!

SEX TIP No. 4
MEN – BEWARE OF WOMEN WITH STRONG JAW LINES AND SEE–THROUGH DRESSES!

SEX TIP No. 6
NEVER BLOW OFF WHILE DOING IT DOGGY STYLE!

SEX TIP No. 7
THE PERILS OF HAVING A WOMAN WITH BIG BOOBS.

SEX TIP No. 9
MEN – TO SHOW HOW MUCH YOU LOVE HER, TREAT HER TO A SLAP-UP MEAL!

SEX TIP No. 10
NEVER BURP DURING A SNOG!

SEX TIP No. 11

MEN – IF YOU THINK SHE'S READY, SHOW HER YOUR CHOCOLATE STARFISH!

SEX TIP No. 13
FOR MANY, MAKING A VIDEO OF YOU HAVING SEX IS NOT ACTUALLY A TURN ON.

MEN – IF A GIRL ASKS YOU BACK TO HERS FOR A THREESOME, MAKE SURE YOU ASK EXACTLY WHAT SHE MEANS!

SEX TIP No. 16

OLDER LADIES – BE MORE ROMANTIC BY HIDING GIFTS FOR YOUR LOVED ONE UNDER EACH ROLL OF FLAB!

SEX TIP No. 18
IF YOU RUN OUT OF CONDOMS, DON'T WORRY – USE WHATEVER IS TO HAND!

LADIES – TRY NOT TO LET YOUR BOOBS BOUNCE AROUND SO MUCH DURING SEX.

SEX TIP No. 20
OLDER LADIES – WHY NOT GIVE YOUR MAN A TREAT AND GO WITHOUT A BRA!

MEN – REMEMBER TO ALWAYS SPEND HOURS ON FOREPLAY.

LADIES – DO NOT KISS YOUR STUBBLE-FACED MAN WHEN WEARING LOTS OF PERFUME.

IT'S NOT A GOOD IDEA TO SLEEP WITH YOUR HEAD BETWEEN YOUR GIRLFRIEND'S BOOBS.

SEX TIP No. 26
ALWAYS CHECK UNDER THE BED <u>BEFORE</u> YOU BEGIN YOUR PASSIONATE BOUNCING.

DURING SEX, MAKE SURE THAT IT DOESN'T SLIP OUT.

SEX TIP No. 28
IF YOU SNEAK HOME FROM WORK TO HAVE A QUICKIE, MAKE SURE YOUR DECOY IS CONVINCING.

IF YOU ARE GOING TO SLEEP AROUND, BE PREPARED TO SUFFER THE CONSEQUENCES.

SEX TIP No. 30
MEN – PUT A SOCK DOWN YOUR TRUNKS TO BOOST YOUR MANLY APPEARANCE, JUST MAKE SURE IT DOESN'T SLIP.

NEVER HUG TOO HARD IF YOU'VE PUT ON BABY OIL.

SEX TIP No. 32

LADIES – IF YOU COVER YOUR BOYFRIEND IN CHOCOLATE, DON'T GET CARRIED AWAY.

MEN – HOW TO TELL IF YOU'RE
GOOD IN BED!

1. THE NEIGHBOURS COMPLAIN ABOUT THE NOISE!

2. SHE'LL AGREE TO HAVE SEX EVEN IF EASTENDERS IS ON.

3. HER HEAD EXPLODES.

KA-BOOM!

4. SHE DOESN'T NOTICE OTHER GOOD LOOKING MEN.

It's so unfair. I wish **I** was bald!

5. SHE WALKS STRANGELY THE DAY AFTER.

What happened to you?

Er, I was riding a horse.

I BET you were!

PLACES YOU SHOULD HAVE SEX AT LEAST ONCE!

1. IN A FIELD!

2. EVERY ROOM IN YOUR HOUSE!

3. IN YOUR CAR!

4. IN YOUR GARDEN!

5. YOUR MUM + DAD'S BED!

6. A PUBLIC TOILET!

HOW TO SPICE-UP YOUR SEX LIFE!

1. TRY DRESSING UP IN VARIOUS OUTFITS!

2. TRY USING CHOCOLATE SAUCE, STRAWBERRIES AND WHIPPED CREAM!

3. TRY REMOVING YOUR SOCKS BEFORE SEX.

4. WEAR SEXY UNDERWEAR!

5. TRY USING SEX TOYS!

HOW TO STAY SEXY AS YOU GET OLDER!

1. LIVEN UP YOUR ZIMMER FRAME WITH ATTRACTIVE LEOPARD SKIN PRINTS!

2. DON'T LET YOUR TEETH SLIP OUT WHEN YOU'RE SNOGGING!

3. AVOID SUDDEN MOVEMENTS DURING SEX!

4. USE PLENTY OF PERFUME TO MASK THE SMELL OF DECAY!

5. TRIM ALL UNSIGHTLY FACIAL HAIR!

6. CUT SEXY PEEKABOO HOLES IN YOUR INCONTINENCE PANTS!

REASONS WHY SEX IS GOOD FOR YOU!

1. IMPROVES CONCENTRATION – AS YOU TRY TO GET THE CONDOM ON IN THE DARK.

2. IMPROVES EYESIGHT – AS YOU LOOK FOR THE CONDOM THAT FLEW OFF IN THE DARK.

3. BUILDS STOMACH MUSCLES -
WHEN SHE GOES ON TOP.

4. STRENGTHENS SPHINCTER -
AS YOU HOLD IN YOUR
FARTS DURING SEX.

5. IMPROVES BRAIN
POWER - AS YOU
FANTASIZE ABOUT SOMEONE
ELSE DURING SEX.

ODD SQUAD titles available...

		ISBN	Price
I Love Beer!	(hardcover)	1 84161 238 3	£4.99
I Love Dad!	(hardcover)	1 84161 252 9	£4.99
I Love Mum!	(hardcover)	1 84161 249 9	£4.99
I Love Poo!	(hardcover)	1 84161 240 5	£4.99
I Love Sex!	(hardcover)	1 84161 241 3	£4.99
I Love Wine!	(hardcover)	1 84161 239 1	£4.99
I Love Xmas!	(hardcover)	1 84161 262 6	£4.99
The Little Book of Booze		1 84161 138 7	£2.50
The Little Book of Men		1 84161 093 3	£2.50
The Little Book of Oldies		1 84161 139 5	£2.50
The Little Book of Poo		1 84161 096 8	£2.50
The Little Book of Pumping		1 84161 140 9	£2.50
The Little Book of Sex		1 84161 095 X	£2.50
The Little Book of Women		1 84161 094 1	£2.50
The Little Book of X-Rated Cartoons		1 84161 141 7	£2.50
Big Poo Handbook	(hardcover)	1 84161 168 9	£7.99
Sexy Sex Manual	(hardcover)	1 84161 220 0	£7.99
The Odd Squad Butt Naked		1 84161 190 5	£3.99
The Odd Squad Gross Out!		1 84161 219 7	£3.99
The Odd Squad Saggy Bits		1 84161 218 9	£3.99
The REAL Kama Sutra		1 84161 103 4	£3.99
The Odd Squad Volume One		1 85304 936 0	£3.99

HOW TO ORDER ... Please send a cheque/postal order in £ sterling, made payable to 'Ravette Publishing' for the cover price of the books and allow the following for postage and packing...

UK & BFPO	70p for the first book & 40p per book thereafter
Europe & Eire	£1.30 for the first book & 70p per book thereafter
Rest of the world	£2.20 for the first book & £1.10 per book thereafter

RAVETTE PUBLISHING   Unit 3, Tristar Centre, Star Road,
Partridge Green, West Sussex RH13 8RA

Prices and availabiliy are subject to change without prior notice.